Red's Eats

Maine's World Famous Lobster Shack

Red's Eats

Maine's World Famous Lobster Shack

by Virginia Wright & Debbie Gagnon

Published by Red's Eats, Inc.

Copyright © 2024 by Virginia Wright and Debbie Gagnon

Reds Eats - Second Edition with added and revised content by Debbie Gagnon.

ISBN: 979-8-218-45099-1

Library of Congress Control Number: 2024913959

Updated design and page layout by Clif Graves / hinterlandspress.com

Copies of this book purchased in the USA, are printed in the USA.
Copies of this book purchased in other countries,
are printed in or near the country where they are purchased.

Joe Devenney

Family, laughter, life—
Dad was the best of all three.
This one's for you, Dad.
You're loved and missed beyond words.

—D.G.

Contents

Foreword by Debbie Gagnon 2

Introduction 4

1 **The Roll of Fame 8**
2 **The History of Red's Eats 20**
3 **Al "Red" Gagnon: The Man Behind Red's Eats 26**
4 **Red's Other Eats 36**
5 **Red's from the Inside Out 48**
6 **You Learn to Love the Line 54**

Acknowledgments 70

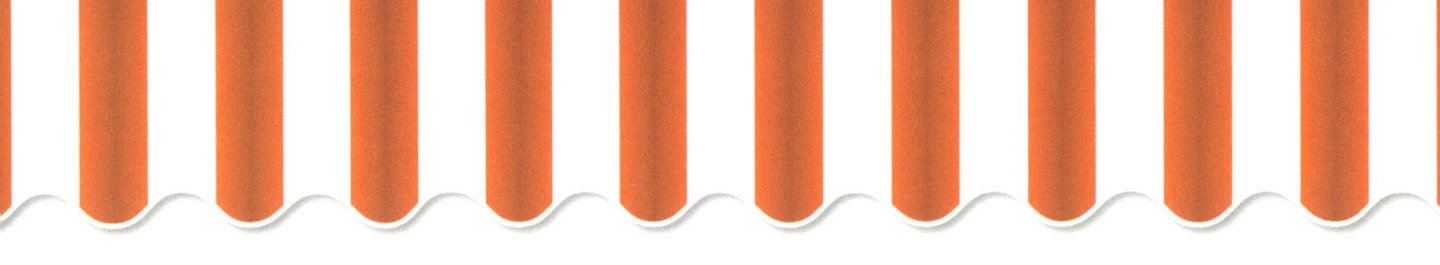

Pat Shannon

Bath artist Pat Shannon's paper collage graces the postcards sold at Red's.

Dear Reader,

Red's Eats means a lot of things to many people. Some are curious, others fascinated, and many are devoted. It holds a special place for many: Their first job . A place to grab a late-night snack . Where they saw a celebrity . Sharing Red's with their children and grandchildren . Where they celebrated an anniversary or birthday . Had their most favorite meal . Met old friends and made new ones . It's nostalgic—it takes people back to a simpler time.

Red's Eats is a true family-run business in this cookie cutter, franchise age. There aren't many of us left. Red's is also a season indicator for locals: The opening of Red's signifies summer is on the way. The closing indicates winter is not long behind.

We celebrate Red's Eats and the man who made it a sensation, Dad.

We salute all the past owners and employees of Red's Eats—we're here because you were. Red's success is measured by our delighted customers and we owe our success to you all. We hope you enjoy the book and learning the history of this great little restaurant that we're so proud of.

Stay well, and we look forward to your visit!

—Debbie Gagnon

"A whole lobster requires concentrated effort to eat, but a lobster roll is trouble-free. It is the simplest sandwich, basically lobster meat surrounded by bread. The best lobster roll on earth is served at an extremely humble shack known as Red's Eats. Red's primacy is a legend among lobster lovers, who flock to it in such numbers (summer only), the wait in line can be up to an hour."

—Michael Stern, *USA Today*

Introduction

The most famous restaurant on Route 1 in Maine is a bit of enchantment on a sunny morning, part summer-stock theater, part religious pilgrimage, all unfolding outdoors in a leafy nineteenth-century village on the bank of a tidal river.

It resembles little more than a red caboose hauled uphill from the railroad tracks and plunked beneath a fine Siberian elm. Despite its Lilliputian dimensions, it is impossible to miss. For one thing, the roof is crowned with a large and distinctively lettered red-and-white sign reading "Red's Eats." For another, there is the line.

A trail of people, dozens of them, winds from beneath the candy-striped awning on Water Street in Wiscasset, and rounds the corner onto Main. Minute by minute the queue grows, spreading downhill toward the bridge that carries Route 1 over the Sheepscot River. Many of these people have planned their entire vacation around this moment: This is their chance to sink their teeth into a lobster roll whose impressive proportions are exceeded only by its international reputation.

Whether it's due to the lobster roll, or the river view, or the welcoming and hardworking family who continue the legacy of the late Al "Red" Gagnon, people are extraordinarily devoted to Red's Eats.

Wearing his Red's Eats souvenir tee-shirt, Duffy Franco, of Norwalk, Connecticut, sits with a woman of the Padaung Hill Tribe in northern Thailand. The photo is displayed next to the take-out window.

The façade and takeout window are papered with photographs sent by adoring customers: Here are the Kelleys celebrating their thirty-eighth anniversary with lobster sandwiches on Red's deck. There is Duffy wearing his Red's Eats tee shirt in Thailand, a long-necked tribeswoman sitting by his side.

The waiting patrons are, for the most part, in good spirits, united by a sense that they are all in this together. They rock from foot to foot and commiserate with each other's road weariness. They admire the river, where lobsterboats putter among brightly colored buoys. They share stories—how they first heard about Red's Eats, how many times they've dined here, and what's good besides the lobster roll.

If the takeout window remains shuttered after the clock strikes eleven, the first-timers in the crowd begin to get fidgety. The veterans, in response, become almost aggressively patient, as if they can impart their insiders' cool to the masses through posture alone. They know the time is near when the refrigerated truck pulls up and plastic tubs of fresh lobster meat are whisked inside the crimson shed's side door. At last the takeout window opens like a velvet curtain on a summer stage, and the line begins to move.

" Don't measure the lobster; pile it high. "

—Al "Red" Gagnon

" This, ladies and gentlemen, is a lobster roll. "

—Ian Jackman, Eat This!

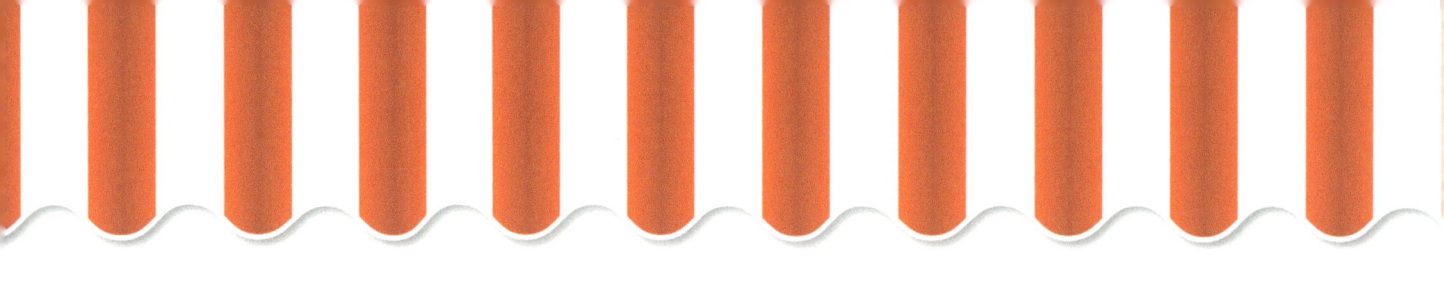

Nance Trueworthy

1

The *Roll* of Fame

If you're on the deck behind Red's Eats, this book in one hand, a fat lobster roll in the other, take a long and loving look at that sandwich because we're about to return your luscious crustacean from whence it came.

But first, a few words about that overflowing mound of sweet, chunky meat in a buttery, grilled cradle. It is the inspiration of the late Al Gagnon, the owner of Red's Eats for thirty-one years. A master cook of simple, comforting food, Gagnon was moved to add the lobster roll to his menu after sampling a disappointing version elsewhere. "I bit into it and—awg!—the frozen meat and what have you," a wincing Gagnon told WQED Pittsburgh's Rick Sebak in 2002. "I said to myself, 'You're going to make a lobster roll that's a *lobster roll*.'"

Gagnon's first effort mixed the lobster with a bit of mayonnaise, a common

From left to right, Red's children Joe, Cindy, and David all worked at their father's eatery.

preparation for lobster rolls in Maine. After hearing the words "hold the mayo" over and over, however, he tried an ingeniously simple new tack: he stuffed his buns with an ultra-generous serving of unadorned lobster, and offered mayonnaise and drawn butter on the side.

"People loved that," said Cindy Collamore, Gagnon's daughter, who worked at Red's Eats along with brothers, David and Joe Gagnon.

Indeed they did. Word of the mouthwatering mountain of goodness spread, enchanting vacationers, whose hordes attracted the attention of food and travel writers, whose rhapsodizing drew morning show hosts and television chefs, whose delirium called forth ever more vacationers.

Behold! In your hand rests the lobster roll known 'round the world.

But how did it get here? To answer that question, we're going to deconstruct your roll and rewind its journey from take-out window to sea. (Relax. We're speaking figuratively. You may go ahead and eat your lobster roll.)

Minutes before your sandwich emerged from the kitchen in its foil wrapping, the day's lobster roll queen—most likely Shannon Brown—was assembling it on a two-by-two-foot square of countertop. Dipping her gloved hand into a plastic container, Shannon grabbed large pieces of lobster, ripped them into chunks (she never,

never, never, ever uses a knife, which can impart an oxidized-metal flavor to seafood), and stuffed them into an expertly grilled split-top hot dog bun. Next, Shannon snugged the meat from two whole claws into the bun so they poked from each end like rose-colored mittens waving for attention. Finally, she crowned her creation with a whole, split lobster tail. Not once did Shannon weigh the meat; her eyes and fingers did the measuring. The average Red's Eats roll contains *much more* than the equivalent amount of meat that can be extracted from a one-pound hard-shell lobster, which is roughly six ounces.

Nate Kauffman

The fresh lobster meat that Shannon piled into your roll arrived at Red's Eats this very morning between 11:00 and 11:30 A.M. aboard a refrigerated truck from Atlantic Edge Lobster, family owned shellfish processor on the water in Boothbay Harbor. Red's also buys lobster from Maine Shellfish in Ellsworth, Ready Seafood in Saco & Shucks Lobster in Richmond, Maine. That meat came from lobsters that yesterday were very much alive, crawling around in Atlantic Edge's holding tanks until they were dropped into industrial-size pots of boiling water. Fifteen minutes or so later, the cooked lobsters were deposited on a table, where three shuckers began snapping off tails and gently cracking claws with hammers to extract the meat within.

The iconic Maine crustaceans had been delivered to the company's docks a day or two

Three Cheers for Red's Roll

"How could you not develop a crush on this crustacean creation? Each buttery bun contains more than one-third pound of sweet, chunky meat and nothing else."

—USA Today

"What a beauty and what a whopper! It appears that all the meat from a decent-size lobster has been extracted in big chunks and loaded into a buttered and grilled split bun. . .
To eat such a lobster roll is no easy task, for pieces of lobster are likely to tumble out and the bread itself will start to disintegrate from the lobster's juices and the melted butter that is used as a condiment. Few meals we know are so deeply satisfying."

—Jane and Michael Stern, Roadfood

"The late daylight was sweet, the stand's name, Red's Eats, was quirky, and the people queued up were really into the food. As one devotee told me, 'Red's lobster rolls will change your life.'"

—Harry J. Lew, Hartford Courant

before by thirty lobsterboats. Perhaps the meat in your sandwich came from the lobsters swimming in the holding tank of *Optical Illusion*, captained by Nick Hawke. A 2006 graduate of Boothbay Region High School, Hawke began lobstering with his dad when he was eight years old and was fishing on his own by the time he was thirteen.

The day your lobster was caught, Hawke and his sternman, Finn Carroll, met on the dock in Southport at 5:15 A.M. to load barrels of ripe-smelling bait—salted herring, redfish, pogies—onto the deck of *Optical Illusion*. By 6:00 A.M., they were motoring out to Hawke's first orange and white buoy, which was tethered to a line of cage-wire traps, each one weighted, baited, and resting on the ocean floor. Working near the bow, Hawke snagged the buoy with a gaff and winched the first trap on board, sliding it along to gunwale to Carroll. The sternman picked out the lobsters, if there were any, banding the claws of the keepers—lobsters that measure between 3.25 and 5 inches from their eye sockets to the edge of the carapace (body)—and tossing the shorts and berried, or egg-bearing, females overboard. Finally, he re-baited the trap and dropped it back into the sea, just in time to receive another trap from Hawke. Once that line of traps was emptied, *Optical Illusion* moved on to another orange and white buoy. By day's end, Hawke and

Carroll delivered the contents of three hundred traps to Atlantic Edge, where they were launched on their journey to your lobster roll.

The Great Lobster Roll Debate

On this most Mainers can agree: an authentic lobster roll is a top-loading hot dog roll filled with chunks of cold, cooked, fresh lobster.

After that, the definition gets fuzzy. Should it be dressed with mayonnaise or butter or nothing at all? Can it be called a lobster roll if it contains celery and lettuce, a sprinkling of smoky paprika or, God forbid, finely diced cucumber, sliced scallions, and tarragon à la chef Jasper White, a self-proclaimed New England food authority (wait—wasn't he born and raised in New Jersey?)? And who invented the scrumptious sandwich anyway?

Good questions all, and knowing how steamed aficionados get over what they consider lobster roll impostors, we're not about to offer definitive answers.

For one thing, there seem to be as many claims to the lobster roll's invention as there are ways to prepare it. One story holds that Harry Perry first served up lobster on a bun in his Milford, Connecticut, restaurant (now defunct) sometime during the 1920s. The long-gone Nautilus Tea Room in Marblehead, Massachusetts, also has been credited with creating the

Nate Kauffman

> **" Red's is almost universally recognized as serving the best lobster rolls on the Maine coast—therefore, by extension, the best anywhere. "**
>
> —Patricia Schultz, *1000 Places in the USA and Canada to See Before You Die*

Ten Quick Bites:

Maine Lobster

1 Lobsters were so plentiful in colonial times that they were considered poor-man's food. Colonists easily plucked them from tidal pools and beaches where they had been surf-tossed by the scores.

2 A female lobster is called a "hen," and a male lobster is called a "cock." A lobster that has reached minimum market size—about one pound—is a "chick," and no, it doesn't taste like it.

3 Most live lobsters are greenish black in color, though orange, yellow, white, and even brilliant blue lobsters have been caught. Lobsters turn red only when they are cooked. No wonder Mainers chuckle over the name of their new NBA Development League team: the Red Claws.

4 Maine landings comprise 90 percent of the nation's lobster supply. The largest harvest on record: 75,298,328 pounds of lobsters taken by Maine lobstermen in 2004.

5 The largest lobster caught on record weighed forty-four pounds, six ounces. It was taken in Nova Scotia. It was between three and four feet long and estimated to be one hundred years old.

6 A lobster pregnancy can last as long as two years. The female carries her mate's sperm for up to a year before releasing and, thus fertilizing, her eggs—8,000 to 12,000 of them—which she then carries on the underside of her tail for another year.

7 Only one-tenth of one percent of a female lobster's hatched eggs will survive longer than six weeks. That's just eight to twelve lobsters out of 12,000 small fry.

8 Because lobsters have a simple nervous system similar to that of insects, neurophysiologists believe they do not experience pain when they are boiled or steamed alive.

9 A one-pound hard-shell lobster contains about six ounces of meat. A similarly sized soft-shell lobster houses about three ounces of meat—and a lot of water. Despite the smaller serving, softshell lobsters have many aficionados, who swear the meat is sweeter.

10 Three ounces of lobster meat contains just ninety-six calories and half a gram of fat. Amazing as lobster is, however, it cannot erase the calories in the drawn butter you drench it in.

sandwiches as a way of making use of culls (one-clawed lobsters). Bayley's Lobster Pound at Pine Point wisely stops short of declaring creatorship, boasting only that it was the first place in Maine to put lobster rolls on the menu. Without exact dates or documentation, we can't say who created this delightful version of lazy-man's lobster, but we're glad they did.

Nutmeggers like their rolls filled with hot lobster drenched in melted butter, but cold or room-temperature lobster is the norm elsewhere in New England. Here in Maine, the lobster roll is most commonly constructed by mixing the shellfish chunks—they should never be mashed to shreds with a fork like tuna—with the merest suggestion of mayonnaise. Serving the mayonnaise on the side heightens the establishment's ring of authority: this is a place that understands it's all about the lobster. Offering a choice of mayo or drawn butter makes the kitchen's grasp of the culinary ritual seem firmer still.

Plus, the hot dog bun is key. Hamburger rolls can't securely cradle the lobster chunks, and sub rolls are so bready they overwhelm the delicate filling.

And don't even think about using whole wheat.

Not just any hot dog bun will do. It must be a New England-style, or split-top, bun whose flat, crustless sides butter and grill beautifully—sort of like Texas toast on a hinge. Grilling brings out the bun's mild white-bread sweetness and warms it just enough to make a pleasing contrast to the cold lobster.

It's when cooks add extras—celery, lettuce, secret herb mixes—that enthusiasts' claws start snapping. This, they'll tell you, is a lobster *salad* sandwich; delicious it may be, but it is not a *lobster roll*.

Look who is talking about Red's

1000 Places in the USA and Canada to See Before You Die, Patricia Schultz
1000 Places To See Before You Die
10 Tiny American Towns you Absolutely Need to Visit, Greg Cayea
13 Charming Small Towns in Maine, Lindsay Cohn
20 All Time Best Seafood Dives, Coastal Living Magazine, Steve Millburg
50 Things You Must Eat Before You Die, Brinkley - Badgett
8 Amazing Experiences in Maine, Sandi Barrett
AAA New England Magazine
A&E Network - Judge on the Food show FOOD FIGHT
AFAR Magazine
amazon.com
Allagash Brewing Company
American Airlines
American Profile, Michael Nolan
American Sandwich: Great eats from All 50 States, Becky Mercuri
America's 33 Best Seafood Shacks
America's Greatest Roadside Restaurants, Susan Burns
America's Most Honored Business
America's Test Kitchen
Foodies 1st - nbcboston.com - Irvin Rodriguez
Food Insider, Most Iconic Restaurant in Every State
Food On A Roll-Columbus Ohio Dispatch & The Washington Times
The Food Network Show, The Best of Frommers.com
Food Network, Samantha Lande
Gallagher's Travels.com - Jeff & Stephanie Sylva
Georgetown Island Travel Guide
German Public Radio, Sonja Beeker
Gourmet Magazine
Great lobster rolls - discover hubpages.com
Linda Greenlaw
hollyeats.com, Holly Moore
Hubpages - My Favorite Lobster Pounds in Maine
Huffington Post,   Constance

The VID (Very Important Dog)

Movie stars may not get VIP treatment at Red's Eats, but dogs do. To corroborate that fact we have the testimony of Deborah and Mike Mullen. *Admiral* Mike Mullen, that is, Chairman of the Joint Chiefs of Staff. (Admiral Mullen was appointed chairman by President George W. Bush on October 1, 2007; he was reappointed to a second term by President Barack Obama in 2009.)

The Mullens made a stop at Red's on a blistering hot day in September 2004, their golden retriever, Grace, in tow. They took their place at the end of a line that straggled all the way to the Sheepscot. They'd had their hearts set on a Red's meal ever since the previous April, when they has passed through town and witnessed crowds clamoring for Red's take-out despite bone-chilling cold. Now they were prepared to sweat it out and discover what the fuss was about.

"The next thing we knew, Debbie was pulling us out of line and taking us to the left side of the building by the door," Deborah Mullen recalls. "She asked about Grace and said she could never leave a dog standing out in the heat. So she sat us down in the shade, got Grace a large bowl of water, and said she would take our order and take care of us quickly so Grace wouldn't have to be out in the heat for a long time."

Debbie Gagnon, we should note, is the ultimate

dog person. She has a special affection for boxers, which she trains and shows, but truth be told, just about anything that has four legs and barks wins Debbie's heart.

That Grace was in the company of a high-ranking navy officer that September day made no difference to Debbie. She didn't know. Mullen, then the 32nd Vice Chief of Naval Operations, was not in uniform, and neither he nor his wife mentioned it. All she knew was that Grace needed water and shade; she provided it.

Touched by Debbie's kindness, Mrs. Mullen asked her to pose with Mike and Grace for a photograph. The following January, Deborah Mullen enclosed a copy of the photo in a card and mailed it to Red's Eats from Naples, Italy, where Mike had a new job—Commander of U.S. Naval Forces, Europe. Debbie added the image to other customer images displayed at Red's Eats.

That delighted the Mullens when they returned, with Grace, to Red's later that year. "No surprise to us, they remembered us," Deborah Mullen says. "In our opinion, a visit to Maine isn't complete without a stop at Red's Eats."

Deborah Mullen, Debbie Gagnon and Admiral Michael Mullen 2023

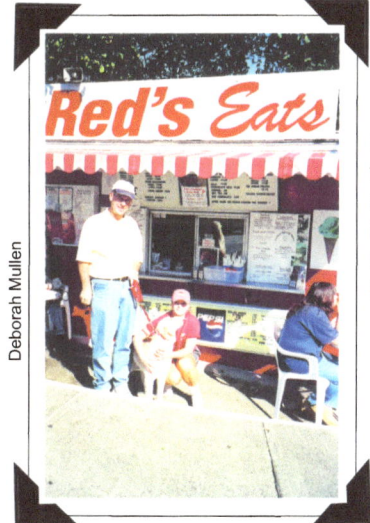

Admiral Mike Mullen, Chairman of the Joint Chiefs of Staff for presidents George W. Bush and Barack Obama, with his dog, Grace, and Debbie Gagnon in 2004.

Red's Famous Lobster Roll

It's true... more than one whole lobster in each roll!

Voted Maine's #1 Roll!

FRESH picked lobster served on a toasted bun. Served with mayo or drawn butter on the side.

... market price

Check out our awards and visitors in our display case!

Nance Trueworthy

Red's *Famous* Lobster Roll

If you want to cook and pick your own lobster meat, plan on one 1- to-1½ pound hardshell lobster or two to three 1- to 1¼-pound softshell lobsters per roll. (Do not use frozen lobster meat; that is a sin.)

- Split-top hot dog bun, sides brushed with melted butter
- Plenty of fresh, cooked lobster meat, including two whole claws and a whole tail, deveined and split
- Kate's Maine Butter, optional
- Mayonnaise, preferably extra heavy, optional

Debbie Gagnon

1. Grill the hot dog bun until sides are toasted and golden. This takes just a few minutes.

2. Rip lobster meat into chunks and fill the middle of the roll. Put the whole claws at each side of the roll and put the split lobster tail on top.

3. Ogle your sandwich. Eat as is or drizzled with drawn butter or mayonnaise. Wish you had made two.

The (Very Approximate) Timeline of a Takeout Stand

1930s
The Little Trailer – Leland and Mabel Bryant

1940s
Phyl and Pat's – Phyllis and Patricia Bryant
The Two Sisters – Evelyn and Francina Colby
The Little Trailer – Stan and Velma Dodge

1950s
Al's Eats – Alan Pease
Al's Eats – Frank Hammond
Red's Eats – Millie and Harold Delano

1960s
Red's Eats – Gladys Light

1970s
Red's Eats – Lola Blake

1977 to present
Red's Eats – Al Gagnon
Red's Eats – Debbie Gagnon, Cindy Gagnon Collamore, Joe Gagnon, and David Gagnon

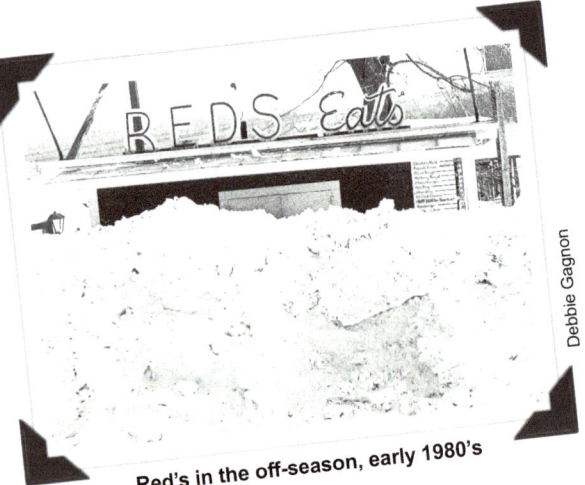

Red's in the off-season, early 1980's

2 The History of Red's Eats

Al Gagnon is so closely identified with Red's Eats, which he ran for more than thirty years, that many people are surprised to learn he acquired his nickname from the takeout stand, not the other way around.

The original Red was Boothbay native Harold Delano, eponymous possessor of the ginger locks. A World War II veteran and Central Maine Power Company employee, Red purchased Wiscasset's little riverside takeout stand in 1957. The hamburger and hot dog joint he and his wife, Millie, operated became a hopping townie hangout, making Red something of a local celebrity. "People loved him," recalls his niece, Lin Delano. "He was full of life, jovial, and happy-go-lucky. There was nothing pretentious about him."

The Delanos had bought into an already established Wiscasset tradition. The concession stand's roots stretch to at least 1938, when Leland and Mabel Bryant wheeled a

More people talking about Red's

If She Wakes, Novel by Michale Koryta
Insider recommendations from the Professionals
insiderpages.com
Indianapolis Star
Jaguar Lobster Run, 2017 & 2018
Japan's Nippon Television Station
Jet Blue Airlines
the kitchn.com - Lauren Kodiak
Landing Home, Susan Birch
QVC-America's largest TV shopping
   network, recognizing our outstanding
   signature sandwich
Rachel Ray Magazine
Readers Digest & Taste of Home - The Best Sandwich in Every US State
Rebound, Kwame Alexander
Richards's Famous Food Podcast
Rick Sebak, Pittsburgh PBS
Roadfood, Jan & Michael Stern
roadfood.com
Road Food Champions 2017
Road Side Stands
Roadster
Rough Guide - Eric Grossman
Route 1, New England, Dan Tobyne
Sandwich America
Sarasota Travel Guide - Sarasota Magazine
Satan's Little Helper, Jeff Lieberman
Seacoast Current.com - Jolana Miller - The Most Historic Scrumptious Fast Food Place From each New England state
Seafood Crush, Tracey Minkin
Sebago
seriouseats.com - J.Kenji Lopez-Alt
amNew York, Rebecca Cooney
Andrew Zimmern, The Zimmern List
Architectural Digest

---

food wagon to the spot beside U.S. Route 1, christened it "the Little Trailer," and began selling sandwiches and soft drinks. A few years later, the Bryants' daughters, Phyllis and Patricia, took over, renaming the business Phyl and Pat's. Sometime later, the place became The Two Sisters. The identities of the original sisters are now a matter of some confusion. By some accounts, they were Phyllis and Patricia; however, Lin Delano grew up understanding that her mother and aunt, Evelyn and Francina Colby, were the ones who first erected the Two Sisters sign. Whether one set of siblings or two ran the business under that name may be lost in history, but, thanks to a photograph in Delano's possession, we do know The Two Sisters had something in common with today's Red's Eats: lobster and crab rolls. The Two Sisters food wagon was eventually sold to Stan and Velma Dodge, proprietors of a pair of clothing stores, the Women's Shop and the Men's Shop, which faced each other across Wiscasset's Main Street. Millie Delano—Mrs. *Red* Delano, that is—managed what was once again called the Little Trailer until she took maternity leave in 1950. "I got a phone call from Velma asking me if I'd like to replace Millie," says Alan Pease, then a nineteen-year-old entrepreneur with a hot dog wagon of his own. "I said, 'Oh, gosh no, but I'd love to buy it.'"

Pease, the future chief judge of the Maine

District Court, single-handedly manned Al's Eats seven nights a week, keeping it open until 2 A.M. on Saturdays when the dance crowd arrived seeking nourishment after a hard night of jitterbugging. In a personal letter from Alan Pease, he said "All during the time I owned the stand, both lobster and crab rolls were a part of the menu. The crab roll's price was .35 cents and a lobster roll was .75 cents.

In the 1940s, what was to become Red's Eats was known as The Two Sisters. The two diamond-shaped signs show that this precurser sold fresh lobster and crab rolls.

In 1954, Pease and his bride, Marnie, opened a second Al's Eats in Boothbay Harbor, but the newlyweds didn't like working apart, so they jacked up their Boothbay shed and towed it to Wiscasset to replace the deteriorating twenty-year-old food wagon. That shed is the same building that houses Red's Eats today.

When he entered his last year of law school in 1956, Pease sold the stand to Frank Hammond, a wholesale distributor of big bait worms that are harvested from Sheepscot Bay's mudflats. Hammond's two sons ran the eatery for a year, after which Hammond sold it to the Delanos, who gave it its now-famous name. The Delanos gave up Red's Eats after five years in favor of a drive-in restaurant on the other side of the Sheepscot. They sold it to Gladys Light, who sold it to Lola Blake, who sold it to Al Gagnon, who put a mammoth lobster roll on the menu and created a Maine icon. None of the owners who followed Harold Delano sported red hair, but all knew better than to mess with a name like Red's Eats.

Seven Quick Bites:
Wiscasset

The Hesper *and the* Luther Little

1 The former township of Pownalborough resumed its original Wabanaki name, Wiscasset, in 1802. The name is variously translated as "coming out from the harbor but you don't see where" and "the confluence of three waters."

2 Once a bustling shipbuilding, lumbering, and fishing center, Wiscasset was a leading shipping port during the latter half of the eighteenth century. Its fortunes declined after the Embargo Act of 1807.

3 Wiscasset's collection of nineteenth-century sea captains' mansions have earned it bragging rights to the motto "The Prettiest Village in Maine," but it was home to a very different sort of architecture for twenty-four years: a domed nuclear power plant on Bailey Point. Maine Yankee, which paid 95 percent of the town's taxes, was decommissioned in 1996.

4 In 1932—five years before Red's Eats' little progenitor, the Trailer, was wheeled onto the corner near the Sheepscot River bridge—the schooners Hesper and Luther Little were laid up alongside a railroad wharf on the river and virtually abandoned. The rotting hulks were arguably Wiscasset's best-known tourist attraction until they were demolished for safety reasons in 1998.

5 Wiscasset also may be the spookiest village in Maine. Numerous spectres have been reported in the town's old mansions. Most frequently spotted is a ghostly old woman in the window of the Lee Payson Smith House on High Street, the former abode of Maine Governor Samuel Emerson Smith. And then there was the mummy …

6 Ah yes, the mummy. An unwrapped three-thousand-year-old Egyptian female mummy rested comfortably in one of Wiscasset's antiques shops for several years until 1996 when a Boston Globe article attracted the attention of a U.S. Customs agent. The ensuing controversy made news around the world. The following year two Egyptologists from the Museum of Fine Arts in Boston declared the blackened and shriveled corpse of no cultural value. It was later sold to a Canadian museum.

7 The Prettiest Village in Maine is also the Worm Capital of the World. Bloodworms, so named for the red body fluid flowing beneath their translucent skin, and blue-headed sandworms have been harvested in the Sheepscot estuary's mudflats for more than forty years. The writhing foot-long creatures, which can deliver a stinging bite, are used as bait by saltwater fisherman throughout the country. Roughly one thousand licensed worm diggers, or wormers, work in Maine. Each bloodworm fetches .50 - .75 cents. Sandworms .30 cents

Down East archive

Joe Devenney

3 Al "Red" Gagnon: The Man Behind Red's Eats

"This building here used to be a trailer," Al Gagnon told WQED Pittsburgh's Rick Sebak during an interview outside Red's Eats in 2002. "It's had quite a few owners. It's been here since '38. When I bought it twenty-five years ago, I kept the name Red's and automatically I turned into Red—with this!" He tipped his cap to show off his silvery hair, then let loose that laugh, the one everyone mentions when they share memories of Al: "YAH-ha-ha-ha-ha-ha-ha!"

Gregarious, generous, and enormously funny, Allen William Gagnon was not the original founder of Red's Eats, but he put the tiny eatery—and some say the town of Wiscasset—on the map with a gargantuan lobster roll that seduced travel writers and food critics across the country and beyond. When he died on June 13, 2008, at the age of seventy-one, his obituary appeared in newspapers from coast to coast. The *Los Angeles Times* proclaimed him "the lobster roll king."

Before purchasing Red's Eats, Al Gagnon sold sandwiches from this pushcart at an area shoe factory. Pictured are Gagnon, his first wife, Ann Sparks, and their daughter, Debbie.

Al "Red" Gagnon in one of his antique cars.

Red's Eats' hold on the summit of seafood shack superstardom was not secured by that lobster sandwich alone. Gagnon's insistence on the deliciousness of everything he served, from hot dogs to fried zucchini, played a role. So did his engaging personality. Gagnon treated whoever was standing in front of him as if he or she were the most interesting person on earth. "My dad was the kind of guy who'd talk to anyone," daughter Debbie Gagnon told the *Times Record,* a Brunswick, Maine, newspaper, in 2008. "He was interested in people, so while they would wait in line he'd ask them questions, start a conversation. It didn't matter who the person was. Whether Paul Newman or a clammer, it was all the same to him."

One of nine children born into a Franco-American family, Gagnon had an itinerant childhood, attending schools in Connecticut and Vermont, as well as Jackman, Biddeford, and Wiscasset, Maine, where he eventually settled. A jack-of-all-trades, he helped build the Maine Yankee nuclear power plant, painted navy destroyers at Bath Iron Works, and walked the village police beat.

He possessed a flamboyant streak and was fond of Lincolns and Caddies, diamond rings, and hearty portions of good food, the cooking and sharing of which proved to be his calling. He began by serving homemade sandwiches from a pushcart at a local shoe factory and catering Boothbay Harbor's tour boats. His four children and their friends clamored to help because he made everything fun. "We would get up at 4:00 A.M. to make sandwiches for the catering business," Lainie Miller, Debbie Gagnon's childhood best friend, recalls. "He'd turn on the radio really loud and start bobbing his head. Then we'd start bobbing our heads, and soon we'd all be singing. He knew how to keep you happy."

When friends questioned Al's decision to buy Red's Eats, which in 1977 offered a limited menu of hot dogs, hamburgers, and fries, he insisted, "I'm going to turn it around." He did, of course, but the revolution didn't happen overnight. Debbie Gagnon remembers many an afternoon spent playing cribbage, passing the time between

BUSINESS WAS BOOMING MONDAY AT RED'S EATS, where owner Al Gagnon cut prices to 15-year-old levels for one day to celebrate the anniversary of the business. He was kept busy serving the likes of 80 cent cheeseburgers at his food stand near the bridge.

> "You can feed anyone once, but feed them twice and you're doing something right!"
>
> —Al "Red" Gagnon

B4 MONDAY, JUNE 23, 2008   ...apolis Star Indianapolis, IN

Allen Gagnon, 71, was lobster-roll king

By Claire Noland
Los Angeles Times

Who makes the best lobster roll in Maine? It's an ongoing debate, but Allen Gagnon had more than his share of advocates. Red's Eats, his modest seafood shack hard by U.S. 1 in Wiscasset, is mobbed by road-food fanatics all summer, with lines of tourists and locals alike snaking along the intersection of Main and Water streets.

Gagnon, 71, died June 13 of respiratory failure at Central Maine Medical Center in Lewiston, but Red's Eats will stay open and the debate will rage on.

Stripped to its essentials, a lobster roll is a toasted hot-dog bun filled with fresh lobster meat. Roadside stands up and down the coast of Maine hawk the summertime staple. Most brush the buns with melted butter, some dress the shellfish with mayonnaise or lemon juice and others add shredded lettuce, pickles or other garnishes.

Many people considered Gagnon's version the quintessential lobster roll. It's a simple bun split and toasted, stuffed with an abundance of hand-shredded lobster meat and served with warm butter and mayonnaise on the side.

A former caterer, Gagnon bought Red's Eats in 1977 and decided to put a lobster roll on the menu after being disappointed by a competitor's sandwich.

Survivors include two daughters, two sons, five grandchildren, one great-grandson, six sisters and two brothers.

One daughter will continue to operate Red's Eats, where a lobster roll goes for $16.50 plus tax.

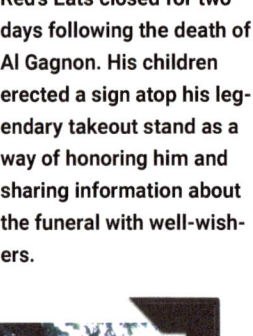

Red's Eats closed for two days following the death of Al Gagnon. His children erected a sign atop his legendary takeout stand as a way of honoring him and sharing information about the funeral with well-wishers.

customers. As word got around about the juicy bacon-cheese burgers, fresh haddock sandwiches, fried zucchini, and other goodies, business grew. With the addition of the lobster roll, it took off like a rocket.

Gagnon usually tended the window or manned the grill. Old Fry-Fry-Fry, as he called himself, worked hard, logging eighteen-hour days. He often stepped away from the fry-o-lators to sit and talk with customers and pamper their dogs (he bred and showed boxers). As the fame of Red's Eats grew, customers came wanting to meet him as much as to sample the lobster roll, and he'd oblige their requests for autographs. "People treated him almost like he was Elvis," says Marie Trottier, who frequented Red's when she was shopping for a summer home and got to know Al well.

Debbie Gagnon

"He'd drive up in a big car, and Debbie would ham it up and announce his arrival. Everyone would be craning their necks to see him: 'Is that Red? Is that Red?'"

Friends and family often refer to Gagnon as an entrepreneurial genius, but he was simply looking to make a living when he bought Red's Eats in 1977, and its astronomic popularity surprised even him. "Al represented a fundamentally Maine way of doing business, [from] a time before franchises when life was a little slower and the folks who worked in the little deli or butcher shop were the same folks who owned it," Maine humorist Tim Sample says. "Al genuinely liked people and he didn't take things too seriously, but he had a lot of pride in what he did, and he wasn't doing it just for

> **Many people considered Gagnon's version the quintessential lobster roll.**
>
> —*Claire Noland, Los Angeles Times*

fun."

AFTER AL
Debbie Gagnon

Manager and Window Person Extraordinaire

In one fluid move, Debbie Gagnon slips a tray crowded with fried haddock and lobster rolls through the window of Red's Eats, steps back, and pulls a microphone from the wall. "We've got a Georgia boy in the window right now!" she trumpets over the PA system.

"Whooooo!" yell her coworkers in a kitchen that's not much bigger than a minivan. "Welcome!" Their whoops and cheers ripple down the line of customers outside. The Georgia boy, a white-haired man in sunglasses, grins and pumps his fist in the air.

Debbie, meanwhile, is already on the move: two steps south to pin the latest order over the grill and two steps west to greet the next hungry customer. "Debbie can

Nance Trueworthy

handle a window like no one else," says Paul Negaard, who embroiders Red's Eats' souvenir tee shirts and hats. "There is nothing that is going to take the smile off her face."

Daughter of the late Al Gagnon, who transformed Red's Eats from local hangout to international phenomenon, Debbie is the summer shack's public face today. She commands the window, stokes the spirits of customers and crew, and greets a steady stream of travel writers and television hosts.

> **The revolution didn't happen overnight. Debbie Gagnon remembers many an afternoon spent playing cribbage, passing the time between customers. As word got around about the juicy bacon-cheese burgers, fresh haddock sandwiches, fried zucchini, ice pops, and other goodies, business grew. With the addition of the lobster roll, it took off like a rocket.**

Seen @ Red's

Many famous people have dined at Red's Eats. They wait in line like everybody else and typically affect an "I'm one of the folks" demeanor as much as anyone can who arrives in a stretch limo and is tended by a bevy of aides. That's what made actress Susan Dey's stop in the 1990s so memorably refreshing. When her order was called, The Partridge Family and L.A. Law star unselfconsciously raised her lobster roll aloft and squealed, "I got mine!" She received a hearty round of applause.

Also spotted at Red's:

Maine Governor John Baldacci
Bear *canine star of The 12 Dogs of Christmas)
Actor Kyle Chandler
Actor Kevin Costner
Actor Tom Cruise
Actress Bonnie Franklin
TV chef Emeril Lagasse
Admiral Mike Mullen (pictured pg. 23)
Actor Paul Newman
Actress Kelly Preston
"The Early Show" weather anchor Dave Price
TV chef Rachael Ray
Actor Robert Redford
Chief Justice of the Supreme Court John Roberts
Maine humorist Tim Sample
TV host and magazine publisher Martha Stewart
Singer Jerry Vale
TV Chef Andrew Zimmern
Phil Rosenthal * Somebody Feed Phil
Monica * Amy from Everybody Loves Raymond
American Singer + Songwriter Lionel Richie

"You never know who you're going to run into at Red's. A couple of years ago, Tom Cruise hopped out of a stretch limo to pick up some hot dogs and an order of fries to go."

—Tim Sample and Steve Bither, *Maine Curiosities*

As a teenager, Debbie worked alongside her dad in his catering business, serving homemade sandwiches from a pushcart at the Eaton Shoe factory in Richmond and delivering dinners to tour boats in Boothbay Harbor. Later she worked at his home-based pizza parlor, Al's Place, and, of course, at Red's Eats.

She inherited her father's love for animals, especially boxers and horses, which she shows. She was one of the horse handlers for *The Man Without a Face*, which was filmed in Maine and starred its director, Mel Gibson.

Debbie managed an Edgecomb restaurant before coming back across the Sheepscot to again work alongside her dad and sister and to manage Red's Eats in 1996. "I'm there every single day, seven days a week," Debbie says. "Especially after losing Dad in 2008, I think it's important for people to see a familiar face at the window."

Al Gagnon pictured above with daughters Debbie (right) and Cindy Collamore (left)

Nance Trueworthy

Hours of back-aching and tedious work in the gathering and preparation, the Harveys' clams are scarfed down in minutes by the pint and half-pint at Red's Eats, where the morsels form the sweet and nutty center of a crispy fried nugget.

Red's clams are about as perfect as batter-fried clams can be, and that's in large part because they hail from just down the road.

Debbie Gagnon

4 Red's *Other* Eats

At low tide, Elizabeth Harvey's brothers, sisters, nieces, and nephews fan out over mudflats of the Blue Hill peninsula in Down East Maine.
Their thigh-high boots sink into coarse gray sand that is the consistency of a New England ice cream frappe, and they bend deep at the waist to plunge fearsome-looking rakes with ten-inch tines into the briny muck. The large clods they turn over are studded with soft-shell clams, which they pluck with rubber-gloved hands and drop into pails and wooden baskets.

Hours of mud slogging later, they take their harvests to Harvey's Landing in Prospect, the small shucking house that Elizabeth owns with her husband, James. A third-generation clam shucker, Elizabeth considers working the shoreline her heritage. Her mother was a Washington State Clallam-Chimakum Indian, her father part Maine Passamaquoddy—both

> "There seems to be nothing that Red's doesn't do well... I'm not a fan of batter-fried clams, but if I were, and thanks to Red's I might convert, I'd rate these excellent."
>
> —Holly Moore, HollyEats.com

coastal tribes. James Harvey's roots are in another Maine tradition, woodcutting, but he has been shucking clams with Elizabeth for nearly twenty years.

Together James and Elizabeth sort and grade the clams by hand, tossing out those with broken shells and gathering the good ones into fifty-pound bushels, for which they pay the harvesters the day's market price. When they have an adequate supply, they dip the clams in boiling water for four or five seconds—just enough to loosen the tough skin around the mollusks' "necks" (siphons)—then dump them on a table to begin the painstaking task of shucking. Cradling a clam in the palm of her hand, Elizabeth slips a two-inch scallop knife between the shells and slides around the rim to cut the hinge muscle and scoop out the meat. She picks up another clam and repeats the process, and James does the same by her side.

Hours of back-aching and tedious work in the gathering and preparation, the Harveys' clams are scarfed down in minutes by the pint and half-pint at Red's Eats, where the morsels form the sweet and nutty center of a crispy fried nugget. Red's clams are about as perfect as batter-fried clams can be, and that's in large part because they hail from just down the road.

There's more to Red's Eats than fried clams and lobster rolls, of course.

Fresh, locally harvested seafood is a theme here. The haddock, served fried or grilled, is landed daily in Portland, according to Jeff Lewis of Mill Cove Lobster Pound in Boothbay Harbor, which cleans, cuts, and delivers the fish, along with the Harveys' clams. The crabmeat, mounded into grilled rolls or shaped into patties and fried, is the sweet and delicately flavored Maine variety.

What's to eat besides seafood? Plenty. Shannon Brown keeps the deep fryers bubbling full time with accompaniments like home made onion rings, zucchini strips, mushrooms, not to mention a sinfully tender, sugar dusted fried dough for dessert. The grill sizzles with Black Angus hot dogs ("the best in New England," proclaims *Boston* magazine) and grilled cheese sandwiches. Even the hamburgers, served plain or with a variety of toppings, are standouts. Juicy and tender, one of these big patties tastes like filet mignon on a bun.

> "As soon as I arrived I got in line to order my own dinner. The woman in front of me was terribly upset that they were out of mushrooms for her meal. The young lady at the counter, Cassandra Fairfield, Allen's granddaughter, was very patient, apologized profusely, and empathized with the woman's situation. I can guarantee that most would not have been so compassionate about another person's"
>
> Douglas Morier on "Good Manners at Red Eats" in Wiscasset Newspaper

Dressed as a natural casing hot dog, Al "Red" Gagnon marches in the Wiscasset Fourth of July Parade with daughter Cindy.

Allen's Children

When Al "Red" Gagnon was away, his children sometimes played. Good thing, too, because messing around led to one of Red's Eats signature meals: the Puff Dog.

"Dad had gone somewhere and I was bored," recalls Cindy Collamore, Gagnon's daughter, "so I started experimenting."

Then fifteen, Cindy dipped a hot dog in batter and deep fried it. "That was pretty good," she says, "so then I tried stuffing the hot dog with cheese, and I battered and deep fried that. That was pretty good, too, so next I stuffed bacon *and* cheese into the hot dog, and that was *really* good."

She announced her invention to her father upon his return. He was skeptical, but one bite convinced him to put the Puff Dog on the menu. It sold, well, like Puff Dogs. "It was very popular," Cindy says proudly, "and it is to this day."

Cindy, along with brothers David and Joey, have worked at Red's Eats since their father bought it in 1977. Red's Eats was Wiscasset's number one summertime hangout. "It was a big gathering place for the area teenagers, which was kind of awesome," she says. "It was the place to be."

Cindy says the work was hard, her father lightened the mood with his sense of humor. They had a routine for their disagreements: "I'd say, 'I quit!' and he'd say, 'No, you don't quit, because I fire you!'" She'd stomp out of the little building only to return to her father's side within minutes, and the two would resume their bantering and laughing.

Now an administrative assistant at Wiscasset Middle School, all of Cindy's children, Cassie, PJ and Christopher have worked at Red's Eats. In addition to the Puff Dog, Cindy put the Yumbo on the Red's Eats menu. Grilled ham and cheese on a sesame seed bun, the Yumbo is modeled after a sandwich of the same name that was served at Wiscasset High School when she was a student. Brothers David and Joe both worked at Red's Eats as teenagers and continue to work at keeping the little restaurant running. Joe has his own refrigeration & heating business (Coastal Climate Control) and keeps all of the refrigeration running smoothly. Joe also installed an ice machine. Brother David and his wife, Debbie, take care of the landscaping, recycling and running errands. They provide Red's Eats with delicious garden tomatoes and zucchini. Last year, they planted over 200 tomato

"Red's is a local landmark famous for its hot dogs, burgers, crisp onion rings, lobster and crab rolls, and even its ice cream—if you spot a kid with an ice cream cone, it probably came from Red's."

—*Fodor's New England*

plants of many varieties. Both brothers are handy with any problem that may arise and have been heroes more than once! David and Debbie's daughter, Ashley and her son, Bryan work at Red's Eats.

Round Top Ice Cream

The secret to the rich ice cream served at Red's Eats is in the eyes and hands of the people who make it. "If we're making butter pecan, we'll add the nuts by hand to make sure there are enough and the machine doesn't crush them," says Gary Woodcock, a retired math teacher who, with wife Brenda, owns Round Top Ice Cream in Damariscotta. "Same with M&Ms and Oreo cookies. It's very labor intensive."

A Maine institution, Round Top Ice Cream was started in 1924 at Round Top Dairy Farm by Edward Denney, who began mixing and freezing cream, sugar, and flavorings in the barn and selling the delectable result from a roadside stand. Over time, Round Top grew to include a wholesale arm that distributes ice cream to restaurants and stores.

The Woodcocks worked part time for Round Top—Gary as a seasonal delivery driver and Brenda as ice cream maker and counterperson—for sixteen years before buying the business in 1987. When the original facility was absorbed by Round Top Center for the Arts, the Woodcocks built a new ice cream factory and parlor nearby on Main Street. It is modeled after the original gambrel-roof barn.

Brenda is the wizard behind many of the Round Top flavors, a few of which, such as Cherry Berry, were born of lucky mistakes. "We thought we were making something else," says Gary of the creamy confection studded with Bing and maraschino cherries and infused with black cherry flavoring.

In addition to fifty flavors of hard ice cream (a premium variety that uses 15 percent butterfat), Round Top crafts soft-serve ice cream, frozen yogurt, gelato, and sorbet. At the Damariscotta ice cream parlor, demand is especially high for Brenda's seasonal creations, such as ginger, Indian pudding, and pumpkin. Of the fifteen Round Top flavors sold at Red's, Wild Maine Blueberry is the top seller.

WHAT'S IN A NAME: THE STURDLEY

There's nothing complicated about the Sturdley—it's a split, grilled hot dog topped with melted American cheese—but the moniker was a puzzle for decades. When asked about the curious name, the Red's Eats crew generally shrugged and responded, "We think it's a New York thing."

We're pleased to report that the mystery has been solved: The Honorable Alan Pease, retired chief Judge of the Maine District Court, is the father of the Sturdley.

Pease owned the takeout stand at Main and Water streets during the 1950s, when the radio comedy team of Bob and Ray was hot. Pease was particularly amused by Bob Elliott's character Arthur Sturdley, a parody of radio rival Arthur Godfrey, and he bestowed the name upon his new product, a cheese dog. Even then, he admits, the reference went over the heads of most customers.

Red's Eats uses Ridgecrest brand Black Angus beef hot dogs, which Al Gagnon considered the best dogs available. The Sturdley today is served in its classic preparation or dressed up with bacon, grilled onions, and sauerkraut.

Red's Cocktail Sauce

This is the scaled-down approximation for a family-size serving. "It must be Heinz!" Debbie Gagnon insists.

☐ 2 cups Heinz ketchup
☐ 2 tablespoons prepared horseradish
☐ 2 tablespoons ground black pepper

1 Mix all the ingredients together and serve.

Red's Coleslaw

Al Gagnon was an intuitive chef who relied on sight and taste, not measuring cups, to make delicious food. The cooks at Red's Eats have preserved his approach, as this coleslaw recipe attests.

☐ 1 head cabbage
☐ 2 large carrots
☐ Mayonnaise, preferably the extra heavy variety, to taste
☐ Sugar, to taste
☐ Apple cider vinegar, to taste

1 Shred the cabbage and carrots in food processor. Stir together in a large bowl.

2 Mix together the mayonnaise, sugar, and vinegar. Taste, and adjust to your liking by adding more sugar or vinegar.

3 Add dressing to cabbage mixture a little at a time, stirring well after each addition. Use only enough dressing to moisten the vegetables.

**Our "no bread" option
Plated lobster with our own garden tomatoes**

Thank you brother David + wife, Debbie
for the garden tomatoes and garden zucchini

A Word on Mayonnaise

Red's Eats uses extra heavy mayonnaise to prepare its crabmeat rolls, chicken salad, coleslaw, and home made sauces. It's also what comes on the side with your lobster roll and gets smeared on your BLT and Big Al. When Red's closes for the season, the crew divides up any extra heavy mayonnaise that remains because this condiment is next to impossible to find in a grocery.

Sold primarily to the food service industry, extra heavy mayonnaise has a higher egg content than regular mayonnaise, which yields a rich taste and ultra-thick consistency. It also maintains its creamy texture and cling when heated. "It makes everything taste that much better," Debbie Gagnon says.

Some stores carry extra heavy mayonnaise, but be prepared to make a lot of sandwiches: It comes in nothing smaller than a one-gallon jar. Various online food distributors also sell it by the case (each case contains four one-gallon jars).

"Red's Eats, al pie de Main Street, lo reconocerá por la cola de gente que llega hasta ahí de todas partes. Tiene fama de servir los mejores lobster rolls (rollos de langosta) en todo el estado, así que ¡tome su número y únase
a las multitudes!"

(Loose translation: "Red's Eats, at the foot of Main Street, can be identified by the line of people who have arrived there from all over. It is famous for serving the best lobster rolls in the entire state, so take a number and join the crowd!")
—Travesías magazine, Mexico

Red's SHOPPING CART

One of the reasons food tastes so good at Red's Eats is that it hasn't traveled far. The restaurant is a micro-economy, whose success radiates up and down Maine's craggy peninsulas.

Fresh Maine Lobster
Fresh Maine Lobster
Atlantic Edge Lobster Co., Boothbay Harbor
Maine Shellfish Co., Ellsworth
Ready Seafood Co., Saco
Shucks Maine Lobster., Richmond

Fresh Native Clams and Haddock
Mill Cove Lobster Pound, Boothbay Harbor
Maine Shellfish Co., Ellsworth

Fresh Crabmeat
Brenda Pitcher, Wiscasset
Debbie Speed, Wiscasset
Fisherman's Catch Seafood Market, Damariscotta
Maine Shellfish Co., Ellsworth
Mill Cove Lobster   Boothbay Harbor

Milk, Sour Cream, Half & Half
Brewer's Dairy, Augusta

Fresh Eggs
Bowden's Egg Farm, Waldoboro

Fresh Sirloin Steaks & Ground Hamburg
Main Street Grocery, Damariscotta

Ice Cream
Round Top Dairy, Damariscotta

Hot Dog Rolls
Country Kitchen (Lepage Bakeries), Auburn

Homemade Whoopie Pies
Glenn B's   Wiscasset
Daphne's Dezerts, Westport Island
Flour Child Bakery, Wiscasset

The Big Al
A creation of Al "Red" Gagnon, the Big Al is one of the most popular items on the Red's Eats menu.

☐ 3 slices of ham
☐ 4 strips of bacon
☐ Jumbo (5-inch) sesame seed bun brushed with melted butter
☐ Mayonnaise, optional
☐ 1 deep-fried boneless chicken breast
☐ Lettuce + Tomato
☐ Cheese

① Grill the ham and bacon until cooked through. Grill the buttered bun until toasted.

② Slather the bun with mayonnaise if you like and stuff it with the meats. Top with lettuce and tomato.

③ Imagine you are on a deck overlooking a tidal river dotted with lobsterboats, open mouth wide, and enjoy.

Kickin' Chicken Sandwich
Lead Chef Shannon Brown is the mother of the Kickin' Chicken Sandwich

☐ Chicken Breast dipped in homemade batter and deep fried
☐ Bacon
☐ in-house ranch dressing
☐ lettuce + tomato
☐ finish with a hot honey drizzle.

① Dip the chicken breast in homemade batter and deep fry

② Grill the bacon

③ Butter and grill brioche bun.

④ Assemble chicken breast, drizzle ranch dressing, add bacon, add lettuce + tomato, finish with in-house hot honey drizzle

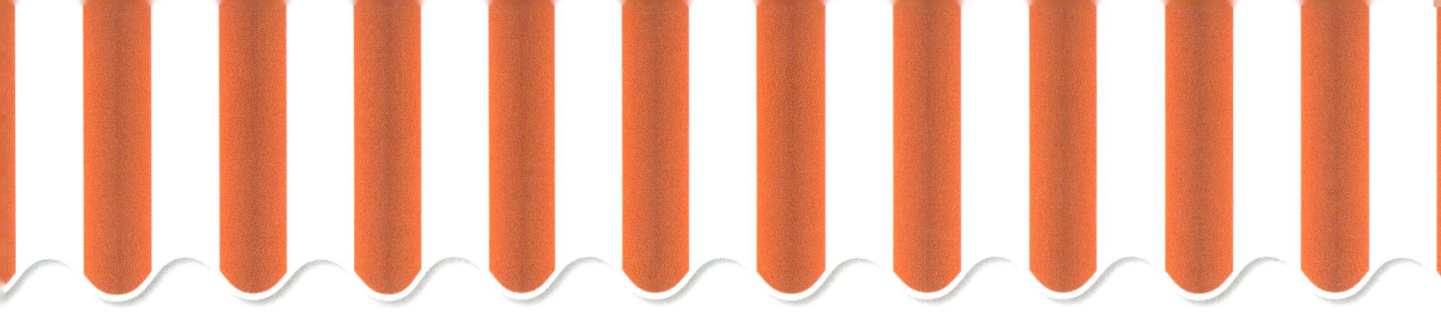

Nance Trueworthy

5 Red's Eats from the Inside Out

"It was cramped, hot, and sweaty, and emotions ran high," Cassandra Bickford says. "It was great."

Cassandra, granddaughter of the late Al Gagnon and daughter of Cindy Collamore, is describing her teenage years working in the fifteen-by-fourteen-foot box that is Red's Eats. "The work was nonstop," she says, "but we laughed a lot and learned not to take things too seriously."

The kitchen is a miracle of efficiency. Not an inch is wasted. On the front wall: the takeout window framed by a pair of refrigerators, with cabinets and shelves above and below. To the rear: a small sink, a placemat-size square of counter for lobster roll assembly, the grill, and a pair of fry-o-lators, one for battered foods, the other for French fries. A few years ago Joe Gagnon installed a walk-in refrigerator and ice machine, and built a walk-in freezer, increasing Red's Eats' workspace by a luxurious few feet.

On the busiest days, which is most of them, five to seven people occupy the thirty-inch-wide aisle that runs the length of the building: the window person, the cook, one or two lobster roll queens, the dishwasher, and two or three prep people, who wash dishes, clean tables, scoop ice cream, soothe the hungry hordes with water and food samples, and otherwise pitch in wherever they are needed. The workers economize their motions. They anticipate each other's moves. There goes Debbie Gagnon, turning to pin an order above the grill, and here comes Shannon Brown, slipping behind her with a lobster roll for the window and sliding away before Debbie swings back. A hand on the shoulder warns, "Freeze! I'm coming through." A tap on the knee means, "Don't move! I'm getting something from the cabinet."

"It's like a big dance," says Al Gagnon's longtime companion, Carol Hutchins, who pitches in wherever and whenever she is needed. "You get so you can feel someone coming and you step out of the way. Nobody has to say anything. They all know what to do and when to do it."

TEST YOUR Red's IQ

ANSWERS:

1. How many tons of fresh picked lobster meat are piled into split-top rolls at Red's from mid-April to mid-October?
   A) 5.25
   B) 8.5
   C) 14.5

2. How many gallons of fresh shucked clams does Red's Eats batter and fry daily?
   A) 2 to 3
   B) 6 to 7
   C) 10 to 12

3. How many pounds of Kates butter are used daily for cooking and drizzling atop lobster rolls?
   A) 10
   B) 20
   C) 35

4. How many employees are working shoulder to shoulder inside Red's Eats during the high season?
   A) 3
   B) 7
   C) 10

5. What is the average length of time you can expect to wait to place your order in July and August?
   A) one hour
   B) forty-five minutes
   C) one-and-a-half hours

6. What is the average length of time you can expect to wait for your food once you've placed your order?
   A) 10 minutes
   B) 30 minutes
   C) 40 minutes

7. How many pounds of fresh crabmeat are served daily at Red's Eats?
   A) 2 to 3
   B) 5 to 6
   C) 8 to 10

8. How many gallons of extra heavy mayonnaise does Red's Eats use daily?
   A) 3 to 4
   B) 6 to 8
   C) More than 10

9. Next to the lobster rolls, fried haddock is a crowd favorite and another popular item on the Red's menu. How many pounds are cooked daily?
   A) 5 to 10
   B) 11 to 15
   C) 16 to 25

10. How many pounds of Spanish onions does it take to meet the weekly demand for onion rings?
    A) 50
    B) 100
    C) 200

1. C. Red's doesn't measure it's servings, but 14.5 tons of fresh, Maine lobster was served last season. It takes 5-6 lobsters to make a pound of the fresh, picked TCK (Tails, Claws, Knuckles) that Red's purchases to make their signature roll, as well as the new appetizer, The Lob Kebop. The Lob Kebop is fresh lobster on a skewer, dipped in homemade batter, lightly fried and drizzled with our in-house lemon garlic aioli.

2. A. The clams are served in buttered, grilled rolls or in pint or half pint boats with house-made tartar and cocktail sauce.

3. C.

4. B.

5. B. Some customers have reported waits as long as two hours; however, they still say the food was worth it.

6. A.

7. C. Red's serves both crabmeat rolls and fried crab cakes.

8. B. In addition to being used as a sandwich spread and in tartar sauce, mayonnaise is mixed into coleslaw and crab rolls. It also is served on the side with lobster rolls.

9. C. Red's serves their haddock as Fish 'N Chips as well as fried or grilled haddock sandwiches. It is delivered fresh each day and each filet is hand cut.

10. C.

Pat Grant
Onion-Ringmaster

The Red's Eats workday begins at 4 a.m. with the arrival of Pat Grant, whose food prep work makes everything run more smoothly.

After taking inventory, Pat gets to work preparing two versions of fry batter—two gallons of extra thick coating for the fried clams and eight gallons of the standard stuff for everything else.

Next she turns to the onions, hundreds of them, which she slices by hand, and the zucchini, which she cuts into long strips, also for frying. She tackles dozens of cabbage heads, shredding them in a processor before transforming them into coleslaw by adding carrots, mayo, apple cider vinegar, and sugar. She brews several gallons of iced tea and iced coffee and makes lemonade as well.

The sister of the late Al "Red" Gagnon, Pat turns seventy-eight in 2010. She used to work alone, but a few years ago happily accepted a helper. Together they work steadily for nearly six hours. Then, when the daytime crew arrives, their job is to get out of the way.

In July and August, the room is an oven, even with fans circulating air. The workers drape damp towels around their necks and maintain the pace. The grill cooks have the hottest job in the house. Iced neck wraps are used to help cool the hard working chefs. It's grueling, nonstop work, yet no one complains, at least not seriously. "There's a rhythm to it, and we've got it figured out," Shannon says. "We have a lot of fun."

THINGS I LEARNED FROM RED

"I learned how to work under pressure and how to deal with difficult personalities. Working at Red's Eats is good training for everything because anything seems easy compared to that."
—granddaughter Cassandra Fairfield

"The biggest thing I learned is how to count back change, which is something of a lost skill today. Also, the way I deal with the public today is the way he taught me: Always be nice to people. Always be polite."
—Shelley Schmal, Wiscasset High School secretary

"He taught me to cook. He had a very specific way of battering items that I still follow: Just dip them in the batter for a very light coating and fry them nice and light."
—Shannon Brown, who has worked at Red's Eats for over 25 years

"He always had some sweet nickname for people and you felt honored to have one. I was 'Llama.' That practice carried over to me and the way I interact with my children."
—Lainie Miller, who worked in Gagnon's catering and pizza businesses

Nance Trueworthy

6 You Learn to Love the Line

Odds are good that you'll meet Jerry Case and one of his Old English sheepdogs (he has six) next time you are at Red's Eats.

Jerry makes the trip to his favorite food stand from his home in Pittston, Maine, seventeen miles to the north, so often that one of the coveted sidewalk tables has his name on it. His arrival is greeted with great ceremony: "Jerry's here!" goes the cry, and out comes Debbie Gagnon or one of her helpers with a Diet Pepsi for Jerry and a hot dog and water for whichever shaggy friend has accompanied him that day.

Jerry Case and Bear, one of his Old English sheepdogs, greet fellow customers.

Jerry and his companion typically hold court in front of Red's for three or four hours. Jerry will buy a BLT or a lobster roll, and the dog will get an ice cream on the house, but the two are there to socialize as much as to eat. "Sheepdogs are fun, friendly dogs, and they get all kinds of loving at Red's. It's good for them," Jerry explains. "The people love them, too. Everyone wants to pet them."

Jerry has six sheepies—Bear, Abigail, Sarah, Emma, Morgan, and Amos. Bear is a movie star, which makes him the celebrity most often spotted at Red's. Once he even came wearing his Santa outfit from the 2005 flick The 12 Dogs of Christmas, in which he plays the part of Yetah, a female sheepdog. You never know who you'll meet at Red's Eats, but do come prepared to make friends and make merry. Red's is one of those rare places in the modern world where most people (by no means all) view waiting in line as part of the experience. They put away their cell phones and get to know each other. It's not unusual to see people who began the day as perfect strangers exchanging telephone numbers and email addresses by the time they reach the window.

"We talk about the lobster roll and whether we prefer butter or mayo," says Holly Moore, founder of the Internet restaurant guide HollyEats.com. A Philadelphia resident, Moore has summered in Maine since he was an infant. "It upset me when some of the so-called foodies started referring to Red's as a tourist trap because of the line. I say they don't know what they're talking about. When you do something well, people line up for it. Besides, it's a beautiful place to stand in line, especially if the weather is nice."

Holly Moore was a delightful, regular customer. After his passing, Debbie created a special hotdog in honor of Holly Moore. The Holly Moore dog is a grilled

A Living **Patio Umbrella**

Wiscasset's pristine sea captain's village charmed Samuel Chamberlain as he considered candidates for his 1948 photographic celebration of American towns, Six New England Villages. The towering elm trees were what won his heart. He remarks on the elms three times in the short Wiscasset chapter, noting their wineglass shape and the way they shield the fine old homes. "Wiscasset's Main Street is arched with elms and lined with good honest Maine buildings," he writes. In the accompanying photo, the road does indeed seem to pass through a leafy sun-dappled tunnel.

Sadly most of those trees, like millions of others planted along other American Main Streets in the first half of the twentieth century, have succumbed to Dutch elm disease, a wilt fungus that grows in sapwood and which is believed to have arrived in this country aboard a shipment of logs from Europe in 1928.

The Siberian elm that shades Red's Eats is one of the rare survivors. Its age is uncertain—elms vary in growth so it is difficult to estimate—but we know it was already a good-sized tree in the 1940s, thanks to Lin Delano's photograph of The Two Sisters (page 29), the food wagon that once sat where Red's is today. The Gagnons are determined to keep their elm healthy. A few years ago they consulted an arborist who recommended that they replace Red's

> **People at Red's are very nice and they are very polite. And their customers appreciate it. Three gentlemen sang me a song one had written to the tune of "Jingle Bells":**
>
> **'Eat at Red's!**
>
> **Eat at Red's!
> Lobster rolls and fries!
> Oh what fun it is to drive
> on Route 1 in July!'**
>
> —Douglas Morier, *Wiscasset Newspaper*

hotdog with bacon, grilled tomatoes, raw onion and Red's in-house bleu cheese sauce drizzled on the top.

Nancy Troop, a Pittston neighbor of Jerry Case, who comes to Red's as often as she can, likes to chat up the queue as well. "I tell everyone that they've never had a lobster roll if they haven't had one at Red's Eats," she says. "I won't eat them anywhere else."

The crew does its part to keep hungry customers' spirits from flagging. They walk the line, offering water, lollipops, and samples of whoopie pies. If someone tells Debbie he's come all the way from Nebraska, she'll announce his hometown over the P.A., and whooping and clapping erupt under the great Siberian elm that shades the rear porch. A friendly competition ensues, as customers eagerly await their turn to boast that they've traveled farther, longer. "It's never old hat to us," Debbie says. "It's exciting and humbling to see all those people. It's important to treat them special. I know they're going to love the food, but I want them to love the other part of it, too."

Red's *Devotee*

Come 11:00 A.M. on the first day of April school vacation week, the traditional opening day at Red's Eats, Marilyn Lane will be in line, wearing her Red's souvenir tee shirt and bearing homemade cookies for the crew.

The Andover, Massachusetts, resident has been a loyalist ever since she started spending vacations at Boothbay Harbor nearly forty years ago. More recently she added the spring pilgrimage to her Red's Eats ritual. "It's well worth driving two and a half hours for one of those lobster rolls," Marilyn insists. "You can't get any better."

She prefers hers with drawn butter. "I smear it on and clog up my arteries for the summer!" she says, laughing.

If there's a line—and there usually is—she befriends the folks around her, asking where they are from and assuring first-timers that they aren't wasting their time. An hour or so later, they'll hail her from the deck with enthusiastic (and well-licked) thumbs up.

But don't take our word for it. Ask Marilyn. You'll also find her at Red's Eats on closing day in mid-October. She's the one waiting patiently for her last lobster roll of the season, a gift of homemade cookies in her arms.

> "Sorry we didn't make it this year. We missed going to Maine, but miss much more going to Red's. The congeniality and good nature is equal to the food."
>
> —Mel and Claire Cowe, Halifax, Massachusetts, in a letter to Red's Eats.

Red's Eats Fan Mail

"In October, 2003, my husband, Con, and I made a trip to Maine for the special privilege of eating your lobster rolls. We were celebrating our fiftieth anniversary. Our son had been here a few months prior to that, and I told him about seeing the *CBS Sunday Morning* show that featured your place. He found your phone number, and I called to find out the dates you were open. My son printed out the info and arranged for our flight and motel. Con was napping at the time, and when he woke up, I showed him the plan. His response was, 'That's a hell of a way to go for a sandwich!' At any rate, eating your lobster rolls was the highlight of our trip."

—Bebe Norman, Whitney, Nebraska

"I am a seventh-grader from Rochester, NY. I visited your restaurant many times during the summer of 2005 when I was in Maine visiting my grandpa with my family. My mother often talked fondly about your restaurant. When I tasted my first bite of your grilled cheese my taste buds went crazy. It was the best thing I had ever eaten."

—Elizabeth Morabito, Rochester, New York

"We came to your part of Maine just for your lobster roll. It's not from Maine. It's from Heaven. You can't imagine how many people from Queens, N.Y., I have sent to your place over the years (about three hundred)."
— Ike Nosomowitz, Bayside, New York

"I again must compliment you on the best lobster rolls ever! They were better than the fancy cuisine I've had in Paris, and I wanted you to know how special you made my visit to Maine for my family reunion."
—Arlene Gilliland, Daytona Beach, Florida

"Mr. Red's Eats: Thank you for the best lobster roll in the world. We have been married thirty-eight years and my husband knows I love lobster rolls, so he found your place."

—Lucille & Bob Kelley, Cambridge, Massachusetts

"We come up every year to your place. Excellent food! We love the fish sandwiches—my favorite. The kids love the onion rings. Great service, and you always have a smile! See you next year, or sooner!
RED'S IS THE BEST!"
—Larry, Denise, Kyle, and Meghan Colvin, Coventry, Rhode Island

An Ode to Red's Eats

After seeing Red's Eats featured on a television program, Donna and Walter Pasiczniak of Uxbridge, Massachusetts, had their hearts set on a lobster roll as they set out for Camden one August day in 2009. When they arrived in Wiscasset, however, they took one look at the line outside Red's and kept going. On their way home a few days later, they pulled into Wiscasset just in time to see Red's being shuttered for the night. Inspired by her unmet craving, Donna, a poet and aspiring children's book author, penned this verse and sent it to Red's. Debbie Gagnon replied with a letter promising a free lobster roll; Donna hopes to redeem it in 2010.

Maine Vacation

So off to Maine we go
My dad I haven't seen
For far too long, I know
Up north, I haven't been

And what a treat it was
Bangor, Bar Harbor, Acadia and more
So pleasing to the eyes
The beauty of its shores

So relaxing was our trip
We vowed we would return
To have a lobster roll at Red's
For this our hearts do yearn

Red's picnic area

More people talking about Red's

Attache, Nathaniel Reade
Austin (Texas) American-Statesman,
   Helen Bryant Anders
Bangor Daily News, John Johnson
The Best Lobster Rolls in America, Coastal Living
Best Lobster Rolls on the East Coast - Forbes & Elizabeth Brownfield
Best Spot for comfort food in America - Chris Sedenka
Best Things Maine
Beverly Hills Chihuahua 2, Twiggy
Bill Green's Maine
Billy Shore Podcast - Add Passion and Stir
Birmingham (AL) News, Fletcher Henry
Blackstone Valley Hogs, 17 Years
Bon Apetit
Boston 25 News - The Best Sandwich in every New England State - Natalie Khait
Boston.com - Best in New England - Shira
Boston.com - Owned by Boston Globe - Back to Back Lobster Roll Champions
The Boston Chronicle
Boston Globe, Janice Okun, Doreen Iudica Vigue
Boston Magazine, Annie B. Coops
Leaving The World- a novel by Douglas Kennedy
Lobster rolls that really rock - Sara Clemence
lobsterfrommaine.com
The Lobstering Life, Brenda Perry
Lobstering Shacks, Mike Urban
Lonely Planet Ultimate Eats - World's Top Food Experiences... Ranked!
The Los Angeles Times
Lou McNally, Maine's PBS
Love Food's Most Historic Fast Food Joint in every state
Maine Cabin Masters   Thx for wearing our hat on your show! DIY Network
Maine Curiosities, Tim Sample & Steve Bither
Maine Food & Dining - Chris Dodge
Maine Icons by Jen Smith-Mayo & Matthew Mayo
Maine-Life In a Day, Susan Conley
The Maine Lobster Book, Virginia Wright

More people talking about Red's

Maine Lobster Council - MaineToday.com
Maine's #1 Lobster Roll   Readers Choice 2018
mainetodo.com
Maine USA - Active Boomer Adventures.com
Maine USA - Active Travel Experiences
Map Guest
Mark Lindsey of Paul Revere & The Raiders
Mashed - The best Roadside Restaurants in the United States
Mavis Butterfield - One hundred dollars a month
Maxim Magazine
Show Me the U.S., Steve McMurdo
Somebody Feed Phil, Phil Rosenthal, Season 5 on Netflix
Soundings, Mary Drake
Southern Living Magazine
Spoon University, Allie Coneys & Megan Jones
Sportsman & Outdoor Channel Network
Stylecaster - Leah Bourne
suitecaseready.com
Susan Bregman - new book, Along Route One
Suzi Thayer, Gagnon Family Story
Taste of the Tavern podcast
The 50 States of Sandwiches - Adam Erace
The Kitchen.comWhere to eat in Maine
The Splendid Table
The Summer I Dared, a novel by Barbara Delinsky
Taste Atlas.com
Taste of Home
Taste of Maine Street America - cookbook
The (Trenton) Times, Kevin Shea
There Are No Moose In Maine (children's book) - Joyce Jackson
Thrillist - Marguerite Preston
Times Record Story, Kathleen O'Brien
Times Union.com - Robin Catalano
Town & Country Magazine
Travel Awaits.com, 12 Best Stops on a Trip from Boston to Bangor, ME

Phil Rosenthal - Somebody feed Phil

Andrew Zimmern - tv chef and author

Aug. 2, 2007
Red's Eats
Attn: Allen W. Gagnon, proprietor
Water Street
P.O. Box 170
Wiscasset, Maine 04578

Dear Mr. Gagnon,

The delay of this letter in no way diminishes the sincerity of its contents.

On June 15, 2007, my husband and I celebrated our fifth wedding anniversary. We also enjoy road trips and try to go somewhere new on each trip we take. We saw a clip about Red's Eats on the MPBN show, Made in Maine. **The image of your famous lobster roll burned in our memories from February until June** when we decided to make the drive to Wiscasset. There was no better way to celebrate than with a true Maine lobster roll.

The service exceeded our expectations. **Everything about that day was perfect from the sunny, blue skies to the sweet succulent lobster and the friendliness of the staff.**

My husband has a gift for gab. Before I knew it, an announcement of our special day was made over the intercom. It was accompanied by the cheers and applause of the other customers. Though I shy away from the limelight, I have to say, this made our day extra special. We were each given a coveted Red's Eats pen and a free ice cream cone **the perfect finish to a perfect meal.**

You have a great crew there at Red's Eats. It was obvious the extra touches came from hearts of people who wanted to create a unique and memorable experience for us.

Some people may think it's crazy to drive three hours for a lobster roll, especially when they are available locally. Just one bite from a lobster roll at Red's Eats and they will know what all the fuss is about. My husband is more of a steak man and even he agrees with me.

We plan to return to Wiscasset when we can spend a little more time. However, we will never return to the lobster salad some call a "lobster roll" ever again.

Thanks so much to you and your crew for making our anniversary special **and for selling a lobster roll worth driving three hours to get.**

Sincerely,
Peter and Janice McIntosh
Old Town, Maine

Debbie Gagnon

Dogs are always welcome. Ritchie is a Red's Eats regular every summer.

Dear Red's Crew,

    Thank you so much for an AWESOME opening day dinner! Elated to see you all back, our town feels complete again.

    A HUGE thank you to Angie for spoiling Dolly Doggo with cookies and attention. It means the world to have a fantastic spot that loves fur babies! Thank you

Wishing you all the best this season and feeling so blessed you are the anchor to our neighborhood.

                Many thanks + tail wags,
                    Lindsey + Dolly Doggo

Red's Eats Loves Supporting Locals!

Maine Lobstermen's Association * Kennebunk, ME
Atlantic Edge Lobster * Boothbay Harbor, ME
Ready Seafood * Saco, ME
Mill Cove Lobster * Boothbay Harbor, ME
Maine Seafood Ventures * Saco, ME
Shucks Maine Lobster * Richmond, ME
Maine Shellfish * Ellsworth, ME
Maine Maritime Products * Belfast, ME
Kate's Maine Butter * Arundel, ME
Bowden Egg Farm * Waldoboro, ME
Glenn B's Bakery * Wiscasset, ME
Dzerts By Daphne * Westport Island, ME
Native Maine Produce * Local Farms
L.A. Tees * Auburn, ME
Ideal Portable Toilets * Wiscasset, ME
The Copy Shop * All printing needs * Newcastle, ME
Ames True Value * Building + Maintenance supplies Wiscasset, ME
Water Lily Flowers * bouquets to welcome new businesses * Wiscasset, ME
Green Bee Honey Sodas * Brunswick, ME
Country Kitchen * LePage Bakery * Auburn, ME
ServSafe class training for staff * Bangor, ME
Burger, Steaks & Ham * Main Street Grocery Damariscotta, ME

Morse's Sauerkraut * Waldoboro, ME
Round Top Ice Cream * Damariscotta, ME
Fried Dough * Portland Pie Dough Portland, ME
Pat Shannon * Artist * Bath, ME
Diane Hammond * Local Artist * Wiscasset, ME
Hood Pros * Winthrop, ME
Johnny's Auto * Box Truck Service * Wiscasset, ME
Chris Jones * Lawn Care & Maintenance * Wiscasset, ME
Riverside Disposal * Chelsea, ME
Veggie Burgers * Jaime Shaw * The Forks, ME
Atlantic Sea Farms * Kelp Burgers * Harvested by local lobstermen & women
Bread Lady Bakery * Dresden, ME
HT Imprints * T-shirts, Hats, Aprons, Yeti * Wiscasset, ME
Coastal Automotive & Welding * Box Truck Service * Wiscasset, ME
Maine Standard BioFuels * Recycling used oil into premium biofuel * Portland, ME
High Tide Printing * Wiscasset, ME
M&R Dorsey Building * Wiscasset, ME
Downeast Audio Video * Topsham, ME
GF Whoopie Pies * Saco, ME
Hinterlands Press * Winthrop, ME
Lincoln County News * Newcastle, ME
Downeast Dog News * Rockland, ME

**Shannon Brown
Hospitality Maine's Employee of the Year**

2024 Red's Crew

Red's Merchandise

A few more from *Red's* photo album

Debbie & Shannon catering our dear friend's wedding

Timothy Rhys

Red's crew

Shannon Brown Hospitality Maine's Employee of the Year

Zhiyu, Grace, Lily and Max

Halloween

Acknowledgments

This book would not have been possible without Red's Eats co-owner and manager Debbie Gagnon, who was unwaveringly cheerful in the face of my barrage of questions about her father, Allen Gagnon, her extended family of employees and customers, the fine points of Red's Eats customs and etiquette, and the picky details of food preparation. Special thanks and appreciation is extended to Nance Trueworthy, whose idea this book was and whose photographs enliven these pages, and to Down East editor in chief Paul Doiron, who recommended me for the project. I greatly appreciate the support and hard work of my editors, Karin Womer, who patiently guided this first-time book author through the manuscript process, and Kathleen Fleury, who buoyed me with her enthusiasm and fun suggestions. Thanks also to my sons, Ben and Otis Smith, my sister Libby Wright, and my friend Shahla Din, who never complained that I spent much of their holiday visit huddled in my office.

—Virginia Wright

I cannot even begin to thank Virginia Wright enough for all of her hard work and talent in bringing this book to life. I will always be grateful to Ginny for making it possible to share the history, fun facts and the story about Red's Eats. Thank you to Down East Magazine for reaching out to me about Virginia writing this book and for making it a reality. Thank you to Nance Trueworthy, beloved sister, for all the amazing photos . You're the Best. You inspire me even when you don't know it. Thank you to Barbara Walsh, dearest friend, for encouraging me, guiding me and for being there every step of the way with my endless questions. You saw the magic and with your expertise and insights, you led me to the reality of revisiting this little restaurant's history with an updated version. Thank you to Clif Grave of Hinterlands Press for all of your hard work, patience and knowledge in making it all happen so smoothly.

I would like to thank all who have recognized Red's Eats in publications, TV shows, social media, books + travel guides. We are greatly honored.

I also want to thank the guests who visit Red's Eats. Your happiness is our greatest compliment and I would not be doing this if not for you. Thank you. Truly.

—Debbie Gagnon

Red's Eats has nestled at the foot of Wiscasset's Main Street for decades.

www.ingramcontent.com/pod-product-compliance
Ingram Content Group UK Ltd.
Pitfield, Milton Keynes, MK11 3LW, UK
UKHW060125240426
12049UKWH00013B/158